Artillery Tactics 1939-1945

Artillery Tactics 1939-1945

by

Shelford Bidwell

illustrated by

The County Studio

ALMARK

Almark Publishing Co Ltd London

First Published 1976.

ISBN 0 85524 254 X

Distributed in the U. S. A. by
Squadron/Signal Publications Inc.,
3515, East Ten Mile Road,
Warren, Michigan 48091.

Printed in Great Britain by
Edwin Snell Printers,
Park Road, Yeovil,
Somerset
for the publishers, Almark Publishing Co. Ltd.
49 Malden Way, New Malden,
Surrey, England. KT3 6EA.

Contents

Introduction to the Mechanics of War

Artillery Tactics by Shelford Bidwell introduces The Mechanics of War, a new series from Almark.

The first four books cover the tactics employed by the three land and the air arms during the Second World War in Europe.

Christopher Chant writes on Ground Attack, Anthony Farrar-Hockley on Infantry, and Kenneth Macksey on Tank Tactics.

They cover the neglected area of small unit tactics which are the basis of every great battle and explain how company, squadron or battery orders were passed down and carried out.

The books give the reader an insight into how the historic strategic decisions of the war became the tactics of the soldier on the ground.

The Mechanics of War will follow these books with a nation by nation coverage of the uniforms, small arms, tanks and artillery used in Europe, the Mediterranean and Russia. Each volume will show how a nation used and modified its weapons and equipment in the light of tactical experience in each campaign.

Acknowledgements

All pictures with the exception of those listed below are from the Imperial War Museum collection. Pages 6, 18, 19, 20, 21, 23, 32, 36, 40, 41, 53, 60, 66, 70 Novosti, pages 24, 49, 54, 56, 57, 59, 61, 62, 63, 68 British Official, pages 12, 33, 51 Almark, black and white diagrams Eric Rose.

Introduction

In 1940 the Germans, after a successful rehearsal in Poland, unleashed a brand new form of warfare. In a short dramatic campaign they swept away the British and French armies; the British to Dunkirk and a lucky escape by sea and the French to utter defeat. This new form of warfare was nicknamed *Blitzkrieg*, or "lightning war", and was designed to avoid the stagnant, artillery-dominated battlefields of the First World War. The men who conceived blitzkrieg tactics had thought long and hard about the reasons for Germany's defeat in 1918 and one conclusion they came to was that wars had to be won quickly. In the first place wars are wasteful in themselves and any political advantages or economic gains in winning are soon turned into losses if they are prolonged. In the second, if they are prolonged then the side with the greatest resources inevitably wins. The only sure hope a country the size of Germany had of victory was to knock out her opponents quickly before they could unite, convert their factories to making arms and their great total populations into soldiers. In the First World War the early victories of 1914 were of no avail when France, Britain, and later the United States, grimly settled down in a long line of trenches, protected by hundreds of guns of all sizes firing millions of shells, to slug it out until they were strong enough to drive the Germans out of France, using the new weapons they had invented – tanks and aircraft – plus guns on an enormous scale.

The Germans saw very clearly that no one could *dispense* with artillery: modern war is, when all is said and done, a matter of deploying maximum fire-power at the crucial point. What was required was some other source of fire-power than the long columns of guns, still in most armies drawn by horses at about 2½ m.p.h., with even longer columns of lorries bringing up their ammunition. (A British field battery used to carry 176 rounds of ammunition per gun with it in its limbers and wagons; enough for one hour's sustained bombardment!) The guns clogged the roads during the manoeuvre phase and the effect of massed artillery fire when the guns had at last been slowly and painfully deployed was to cause everyone to dig in and led to a general tactical deadlock. The blitzkrieg did not altogether do away with ordinary artillery, which was far too useful for a number of tasks, but it employed tanks for some field artillery tasks and strike aircraft – the famous Stuka divebombers – instead of heavy artillery. The blitzkrieg was, in short, mobile fire-power, and the blitzkrieg formula depended on tanks, infantry, artillery, engineers, reconnaissance troops (the successors of light cavalry) and strike aircraft all working together in a team, each supporting the other, with the master weapon the tank. To understand artillery, which returned in a somewhat different form to dominate the battles of the Second World War, we must first understand how the tank evolved from its

A Soviet 152 mm Gun-Howitzer Model 1937 in action during the fighting in Danzig in 1945. This weapon had a maximum range of 18,888 yards and fired a 96 lb shell.

A 6 pdr anti-tank gun in action in North Africa. The 6 pdr had a muzzle velocity of 2,700 feet per second and could penetrate 68 millimetres of armour at 1,000 yards.

artillery ancestor. So we must first look at its history.

Until 1914 artillerymen tried to deploy their guns in mass as close as possible to their targets and in full view of the enemy, regardless of risk. Obviously the shorter the range the easier it is to pick up the target, the easier it is to hit it, and the closer together the guns are deployed the easier it is to control them in combat. Napoleon's great victories were based on this simple theory. (So were Nelson's. The secret of success of the old Royal Navy was seamanship, which enabled a closely-packed fleet of what were no more than floating batteries driven by sails to bring mass fire to bear at ranges of 100 yards or less.) Then it was realised that as weapons increased in efficiency the front line was no longer a safe place for artillery in battle. In the South African War the Boer marksmen, who with their rifles could hit a man at 1,000 yards, cut down the British artillerymen round their guns and also the horses sent up to withdraw them. "Indirect fire", that is fire from behind cover at long range, already a possibility, came gradually to be seen as a necessity. Finally, in 1914, it proved suicidal to put artillery in view of the enemy. It was not only the fire of modern rifles and machine guns which settled the question: the guns themselves had become so much more effective; the suicide was mutual. They shot faster and were much more accurate. High explosive shells and timed shrapnel (an efficient man-killer, especially against the dense infantry formations of 1914, but obsolete by 1939) were more effective than the iron shot and gunpowder filled shells of the smooth-bore artillery of the nineteenth century. If face to face at 1,000 to 2,000 yards the rival batteries simply shot each other to bits. This is what happened at the famous Battle of Le Cateau, where the Royal Artillery lost a number of guns and won a few Victoria Crosses; "magnificent but not war", like the charge of the Light Brigade.

The consequence was that all artillery took advantage of the range of the new guns and their panoramic optical sights to retire from the forward edge of the battlefield to take cover in valleys behind, and use the new technique of "indirect fire" by which observers in front signalled their orders back to the hidden guns. This had great advantages and disadvantages, which will be explained in a moment, but one of the disadvantages was the disappearance of mobile horse artillery, which could gallop through enemy fire, rapidly deploy and dispose of some small but vital target like a bunker or a pill box with a burst of fire at range so short that the gunners could not miss. This want was filled, by chance

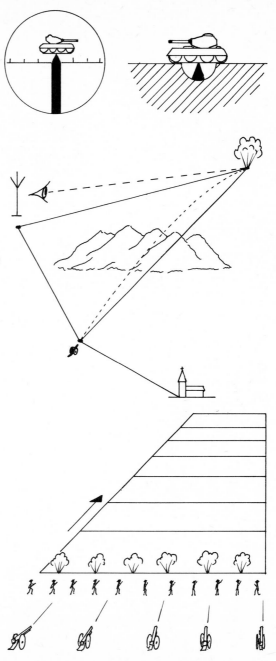

Top: The direct fire view of a target, a tank as an anti-tank gunner might see it in his sights.

Centre: Indirect fire using an observer. The gun crew receive corrections for its fire from the unseen observer and relate these to bearings on an aiming post or visible object like a church.

Bottom: The barrage as employed during World War I. The infantry would advance behind a line of bursting shells.

The blitzkrieg in action in Russia. A German soldier riding on a PzKw III takes aim at a suspected sniper.

rather than by design, by the tank, which was invented to cross the deep trenches of the earlier war, crush wire and help the infantry on with its fire.

One way of looking at a tank was that it was a horse artillery gun, with a petrol motor and tracks instead of a "one horse-power horse" with legs, and with the gun crew protected by armour. This was not the whole story, by any means. The tank proved a marvellously all-round weapon in its own right. It combined the functions of horse artillery and cavalry in the attack; it could give close support to infantry; and in the defence it could provide a row of mobile pill boxes and a swift counter-attack force. Its moral effect in the early days was very great. To face a tank attack is still terrifying for green troops and a test of nerves for the best.

The idea of the blitzkrieg was to burst through the front in several places, the tanks first playing the part of artillery, then close range assault vehicles and finally pursuing light cavalry, spreading dismay and disruption in the rear areas, where one of the chosen targets was the concealed enemy guns. As for the future of indirect fire artillery, the great high-priest of tank warfare, Basil Liddell Hart, considered that it would be of little use except for supporting infantry in wooded or mountainous areas where tanks could not fight, and to help protect the "tank harbours" where the armoured troops rested, refuelled and re-armed. So firm a grip did this doctrine obtain

A 2 pdr anti-tank gun on the back of a truck. The gun had a muzzle velocity of 2,600 feet per second and could penetrate 58 millmetres of armour at 250 yards.

that at one important British exercise in 1942 the armoured division commander sent his mechanised artillery to the rear when the main tank battle began, in case they got in the way! As for anti-tank guns, the out-and-out tank men didn't believe that artillery could face tanks: its role would be limited at best to self protection. The only answer to a tank was believed to be another tank.

Another severe blow to the status of artillery was the initial success of the Japanese in the opening rounds of the war in South-East Asia, where their excellent infantry routed the British and captured all their guns using themselves only light artillery support. Guns, in British opinion, were therefore of little use in modern, armoured warfare and little use in jungle; two rash assumptions which experience was sharply to contradict.

The outlook for the artillery in 1940-1 was, therefore, dismal. Its science, so highly developed by the French, Germans and British in 1918, was allowed to decay. Then a natural law which governs military evolution began to assert itself; this was that a new weapon rapidly generates a counter-weapon, and so on. The tanks had to take serious notice of guns, the infantry proved indispensable and demanded artillery support, the gunners had to learn how to cope with tanks. Above all, the artillery had to rediscover its science and at the same time speed up its techniques so as to keep pace with the blitzkrieg.

A 10.5 cm leFH 18
(M) in action in
Russia. In the
foreground the crew
are setting the fuzes.
The 10.5 howitzer
fired a 33 lb shell
11,675 yards, but this
was later increased
to 13,500 yards.

How Artillery Works

The first question that must be answered is, what is artillery for? Then we must understand how it works, for only then can we understand the part it played in the great battles of the Second World War. The real artillery weapon – the shell – is basically a very simple one. It is a stout steel cylinder with a pointed (ogival) nose, made to spin so that it goes point first; inside is a charge of high explosive (HE) which is made to explode in the air, just as it touches the ground or after penetration, according to choice, by fitting an appropriate fuse. The steel case shatters into hundreds of small man-killing splinters, and the HE explosion can be used to damage trenches, buildings or tanks. Shells could also be used to lay smoke-screens, to conceal movement, and to blind artillery observers and aimers of small arms fire. It should be noted that although artillery is a terrible weapon it achieves far more by the threat of death or wounds than by actual killing. It forces men and tanks to take cover and act circumspectly, interferes with their plans, frightens them, depresses their morale (nothing is more exhausting than sitting out a long bombardment even in safety; the noise alone is a strain on the nerves), and denies open ground to the enemy, even tanks which can be severely harassed and possibly stopped by shell-fire.

In the attack artillery fire is first used for *preparation*, that is a preliminary softening up bombardment of the enemy positions with the aim of causing casualties, damaging weapons and reducing morale. It does give away the point of attack, so the preferred method is *covering fire* whose aim is *neutralisation* (or *suppression fire*), i.e. to deter the defenders from looking out or manning their weapons during the bombardment while the attackers move in to close quarter fighting. In the defence artillery fire may be used for *counter-preparation* to hit the attackers in their forming up places, but is principally used for *defensive fire,* which is a curtain or barrage of fire brought down on the routes by which the attackers are expected to come.

Many thousands of rounds of *harassing fire* were expended by the British during the latter period of the war when their artillery arm was its strongest. The waste was seldom worth the cost, the general idea being to shoot up the rear areas at night so as to interfere with supply convoys and ration parties and to prevent sleep. Against tough troops like the Germans it bred a contempt for artillery fire and it also helped green troops to become accustomed to shelling.

The most scientific and the most important artillery task after covering fire was *counter-bombardment,* the target being the enemy artillery; the unseen fighting the unseen, using every modern scientific aid to locate and neutralise the enemy guns. (These technical terms are all the British ones from the

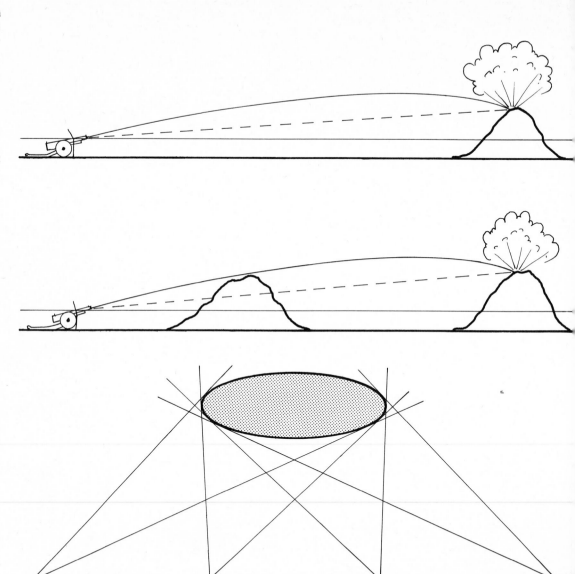

Top: Direct fire, the gun can be layed on the target which is in line of sight.

Centre: Indirect fire, the gun is behind cover of a hill and lobs its shells over the top.

Bottom: The target engaged by different guns using indirect fire methods. (See also page 17).

contemporary manuals, but the basic use of artillery was the same in all armies.)

Anti-aircraft fire was an artillery responsibility, its aim was to protect the fighting troops and rear installations from air attack.

More important from the tactical viewpoint was *anti-tank* artillery, a role for both field artillery firing direct and specialist anti-tank guns.

Having had a short military history lesson, the reader must be prepared for a brief lesson on the science of artillery. It will be quite painless! – indeed, why not? In the war it was learnt rapidly by a spectrum of gunners ranging from educated westerners to Russian and Asian peasants who, when enlisted, were often illiterate.

The process of aiming at a target invisible from the guns was quite simple. First there was the question of finding the range. When firing "direct", i.e. so the gunlayer could see the target, he first pointed the gun at the target and then "cocked it up", or "elevated" the barrel above the line of sight from gun to target to allow for the pull of gravity on the shell, which caused it to fly in a parabolic curve. The range was found with a range-finder or more usually estimated by eye, and set on scale on the sights. When he could not see the target these vertical angles (or "tangent") were worked out from a map and applied to the sights; the basis of measurement being a spirit level. The direction of fire was laid out by compass bearing, the sight being so designed that it would also record horizontal angles. The telescope was then laid on a reference object such as a church tower or a post stuck in the ground. The layer simply followed his orders and set the range and angle to bring the gun pointing at the target. This crude method never enabled the gun to hit the target with its first shot, but the forward observer would see the explosion of the shell and using a telephone

or, more commonly towards the end of the war, a voice radio, gave out fresh orders, until a hit was obtained, by trial and error. It was a much quicker process than it sounds, given a good observer and well-trained layers, and infantry mortars still use it. It was sufficient to range or "adjust" one gun: the remainder of the guns in the battery were kept parallel and could follow suit.

The observer was a particularly important person, although he was often a young captain or even a lieutenant. He was required to understand exactly what support the infantry or tanks wanted, to read the "battlefield" and to engage targets very quickly. In particular he

The commander of a battery of Italian Obice da 105/14 awaits orders on 22 September 1944.

Top and Centre: The mean point of impact see in plan and profile. The greater density of shells fall on the target, but a "beaten zone" or "50 per cent zone" is formed by those shells that fall just short or beyond the target.

Bottom: An air burst. Against dug in infantry the air burst was the most effective form of artillery fire.

Far right: The "50 per cent zone" in relation to the gun. Below is the effect of a shell bursting on the ground. Though some of the blast and fragments go up, a large amount is absorbed by the ground.

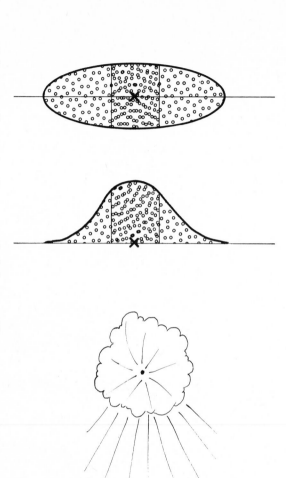

had to look out for artfully sited machine-guns, which could cause terrible casualties among the infantry if they were in the open, or anti-guns. (For it was soon found that high-velocity guns sited in "defilade", i.e. firing obliquely from behind a hayrick or a house, were as dangerous to tanks as machine-guns to infantry). He had therefore to be tactically trained, quick-witted, and be able to make the rapid mental calculations required for converting his view of the shell-burst and the target to the corrections required to be put on the gun-sights, often when he was under fire himself. Today this process is aided by laser range-finders and computers, but it would be interesting to have a competition between an observer of the 1940s and modern methods. They were astonishingly "good shots" through constant practice, and to see one pick up a target with his field-glasses, pour a string of staccato orders down his radio and rapidly smother it in 25 pdr shell bursts was a revelation. It was a poor battery which could not bring effective fire to bear in under ten minutes; in some only five was allowed.

One essential difference between short range, direct fire and long range, indirect fire is that all the inherent inaccuracies due to minute differences in manufacture, sight-setting, the wind and weather and so on have a very much greater effect. A hundred successive shots map out a characteristic pattern, dense in the middle and thin at the edges; at, say, 10,000 yards this might be 400 yards long and perhaps 10 wide, with 50 shell-bursts concentrated into 100 yards astride the point of lay. It is only at 1,000 yards that such a gun could hit, say, a house with the first shot and then not for certain. However, *the degree of inaccuracy is predictable,* so the artilleryman obtains his effect by adjusting fire until his "mean point of impact" coincides with the target, and all these thin, elliptical patterns of fire (what machine gunners aptly call the

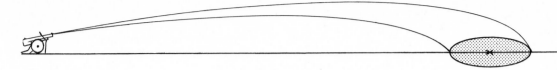

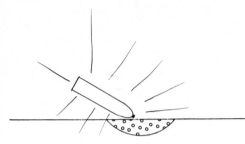

the grid frame of reference on an ordinary British Ordnance Survey map. By this means orders to engage any target could be conveyed to any battery and data to engage it rapidly calculated.

"beaten zone", gunners more mathematically the "50 per cent zone") overlap.

But this disadvantage is set off by an advantage immeasurably more important. By standing back from the battle-front a widely dispersed force of guns can be assembled out of sight so as to obtain surprise and also, by a simple turn of the layer's bearing hand-wheel, batteries miles apart can readily concentrate their fire on to a single target as indicated by an observer from far in front.

This demanded two further techniques, which were perfected in the First World War but required streamlining and speeding up in the Second World War. The guns (batteries, to be precise, because the six- or eight-gun batteries could easily be fixed so as to fire as if only one gun), and the targets had to be placed on a freshly made map; not the ordinary kind of map but one composed simply of points hastily plotted as the battle developed, each representing a battery position and its cluster of potential targets, related to a "grid" exactly corresponding to

A Soviet gunner at the sights of his 76.2 mm Field Gun Model D2/03 in a camouflaged position on the Kalinin Front.

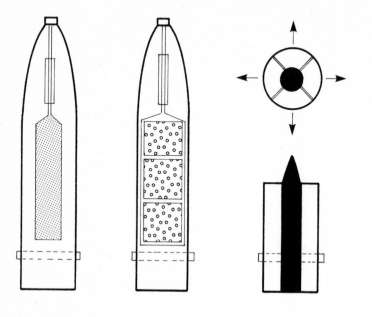

the guns on the grid" was streamlined so that it could be done in hours, not days or weeks. The other, which revolutionised all the tactics described in this series, was the introduction of portable voice-radios, which enabled everyone (tanks, infantry and gunners) to talk to each other.

Finally there was another highly technical ballistic process which had also to be adapted from the 1917-18 period and speeded up to meet the demands of blitzkrieg warfare. All the methods described so far demanded preliminary "ranging" or "adjusting" fire (the former term is British, the latter American; both mean the same thing) to make certain that the pattern of fire of all the batteries engaging coincided with the target. It was an iron rule, moreover, that however good the survey of the grid, fire which was primarily designed to protect the infantry and tanks had to be "guaranteed", which demanded this essential preliminary check. But ranging could give away the *schwerpunkt* of the impending attack and the Germans, who were excellent tacticians (probably the best in history), soon learned how to exploit this information by thinning out in the target area and holding their counter-attack troops out of range ready to hit back at the assault troops at the very moment when they were most vulnerable – when they arrived disorganised and exhausted on the objective after a hard fight.

The demand therefore was for reliable "predicted" fire. This required the following, as well as the mapping, or survey, process described above. (1) Intense intelligence scrutiny of the enemy positions, of which the most fruitful was air photography – the Royal Air Force becoming wizards at interpretation and the artillery surveyors adept at deriving mathematically the grid position of what was discovered on the photograph to within a few yards. (2) "Meteor" or weather telegrams. These were circulated every three or four

All this was perfectly well known and in use by 1918. The printing presses of the Royal Engineers ran off beautiful 1:25,000 maps (still to be seen) showing every detail of German trenches and gun positions, but they took months to make, and all the passage of information had to be passed by a fragile web of field telephone cables, which were frequently cut by shell-fire or tanks running over them when they were needed most. At the crisis of many of the battles of that war the forward observers were out of touch with their guns. Two very important developments made possible the new artillery tactics of the Second World War. The whole process of "putting

A U.S. Army 8 inch Howitzer M1 in northern Europe in 1944. The 8 inch howitzer had a range of 18,510 yards and fired a 200 lb shell. The M1 had a reputation for accuracy and was an excellent anti-fortification weapon.

Far left: Shells, HE, Shrapnel and APDS. The APDS was the British solution to penetrating armour with a shell of acceptable weight. A relatively large calibre gun was used to fire small light shot of low cross section, made of super hard metal. To fit the bore it was enclosed in a jacket of light alloy segments, these "sabots" flew off when the shot left the bore. Hence "Armour-Piercing Discarding Sabot", or APDS.

hours giving the wind speeds, barometric pressure and temperatures at various heights to enable the true trajectory of the shells to be calculated – this could differ from the ideal by as much as 400-500 yards. (Shells from a light field gun at its normal range may rise as high as 4,000 feet, from a long range gun some 18,000 feet.) (3) Measurement of the muzzle velocity *of each gun involved* (and there were 72 in a British, 48 in a US division, not counting reinforcing artillery). Every gun loses range as it wears out and at a different rate, so each gun required an individual correction. In all the stresses and turmoil of a mobile operation the command post officers had constantly to measure the changes in velocity by various means and keep elaborate records. The highly

practical US gunners got round this by the lavish method of frequently changing barrels in action as they wore out, something the British could not afford to do. (Nor were these corrections merely finicking. Some 8th Army gunners scorned such refinements and in Italy one gun was found shooting a mile and a half short, to the alarm and irritation of the infantry whose complaints brought the matter to light. Not surprisingly, for the infantry, who will dourly put up with any amount of enemy bombardment without complaint, object violently to being shelled from behind.)

As we shall see, these techniques were only revived in the British army late in 1942 at the Battle of Alamein; but Alamein was virtually a modernised version of the battles fought in

France in August 1918. It took weeks of preparation to enable some 1,000 guns to open simultaneously at predicted fire at zero hour. In later battles, including sub-battles of Alamein proper like Operation Supercharge, 24 hours was enough to prepare one of these colossal hammer-blows.

To summarise, what was developed was a highly flexible artillery arm with a whole gamut of responses to the tactical needs of the arm supported – whether it was infantry, or tanks, or more usually a combination of the two. For the quick, fluid battle the observer in front could intervene in a matter of minutes with the four or eight guns at his disposal; for something tougher, with his whole regiment (US battalion) or more; while for a big set

Above: The crew of a Soviet 76.2 mm Field Gun Model 1939 (76-39) snatch a meal in the winter of 1943. The 76.2 Model 1939 gun had an anti-tank capability, but could fire up to 14,540 yards.

Right: A Russian observation post. One officer is using the scissor type binoculars known in the Russian army as "Donkey's Ears".

piece battle, when enemy resistance had hardened, he could lay on a great programme of fire as complicated as a railway timetable and involving the most delicate ballistic calculations produced as a matter of drill in less time than it took to make all the other preparations. The iron rule for the Royal Artillery was that it should never ask the infantry to delay zero hour while it elaborated its arrangements.

So far we have been talking about British artillery, because by force of circumstances – neglect to develop a tank arm and a proper doctrine for its use, and the time taken to modernise an infantry arm designed in reality for colonial policing purposes – the British came eventually to rely very heavily on their guns and gunners to hold the ring. The United States army was far more orthodox, and by the time it entered the war had a sound doctrine and an artillery arm second to none in efficiency.

The Russians had a totally different approach. They believed traditionally in the supremacy of artillery – "Artillery is the God of War", Stalin pronounced – and their theory was as good as any other nation; however the need to make good the terrible losses inflicted by the Germans and the backwardness and illiteracy even of many of NCO rank (some could not even tell the time, let alone own a watch) dictated that only the simplest and crudest methods could be used. The battery commander was often the only man capable

Russian 122 mm Field Howitzers Model 1938 are readied for action in the fighting by the 2nd Ukrainian Front near Jassy. This howitzer could fire a 47 lb shell up to 12,909 yards. The Germans used captured M 1938's which they designated 12.2 cm sFH 39(r).

Russian 152 mm Gun-Howitzers dug in during the summer of 1943. This gun was also mounted on the SU-152 and JSU-152 as an assault gun and relied on the weight of its shot rather than muzzle velocity as an anti-tank gun.

of carrying out the necessary calculations (like the British in the earlier war). He manned the observation post which was also his command post (US "fire direction center") and each battery was registered in individually. Attacks were preceded by huge bombardments from guns assembled almost wheel to wheel. In short, technically the Red Army was at the same level as the British at the time of the Battle of the Somme 1916. To say this is not to disparage one of the world's greatest artillery arms; in war one has to make do with the materials one is given. Russian tactical handling was to prove sound, especially when it came to finding a solution to the problem of defeating the blitzkrieg.

The Weapons

Each of the four great armies in the period had a similar family of weapons for field use – defining the word "field" as rifled cannon whose role is the support of the field army. "Guns" are strictly long, high velocity flat trajectory weapons with long range but poor accuracy at long range, while "howitzers" are of larger calibre and relatively (weight for weight) more accurate, and have curved, variable trajectories. In the Second World War the distinction became blurred and the British actually described their new equipment as "gun-howitzers", having the characteristics of both. The only "pure" guns (apart from anti-aircraft) were designed for anti-tank work, where high penetrating power and great accuracy at short ranges was essential. "Mortars" are low-velocity smooth-bore weapons, with trajectories lying between 45° and the vertical, delivering a finned bomb. The biggest are sometimes rifled and resemble howitzers. They were used by infantry. Only the Russians used their powerful heavy mortars in the artillery arm.

The basic gun of the Germans and the Americans was the 105mm howitzer; both very good guns. The British after considering a 105mm howitzer in the early 1930s settled for the hybrid 25 pdr (3.45in, or 88mm). The Russians preferred to have a mixture of guns and howitzers. Their 76.2mm gun was, fortunately for them, an excellent anti-tank gun as well; so much so, in fact, that the Germans adapted hundreds of captured guns for their own ammunition and used them as anti-tank guns. They also had a 105mm howitzer. These guns are all rather small by present day standards, but it must be remembered that they were designed as man-killers, and for suppressive fire on infantry defended localities; a task for which many small shells giving a dense pattern are more efficient than a few large bursts. Also the Germans and the Russians relied almost entirely on horse traction for light field artillery throughout the war; this limited the total weight of limber (caisson) and gun.

A 76.2 mm Field Gun Model 1942/SiS 3 (76-42) in action in the spring of 1945. The Model 1942/SiS was a handy gun which weighed a little over one ton, had a range of 14,540 yards and fired a 13.69 lb shell.

A 40 mm Bofors anti-aircraft gun in position in southern England in 1944. The Bofors was one of the most widely used guns during the war. It could fire about 60 to 90 rpm and was hand loaded with four round clips.

For artillery counter-bombardment, attacking bunkers, pill boxes and earthworks, harassing (and even destroying) armour, and generally lending range and punch to the lighter field guns, the other major members of the family were what the British term "mediums" – the German 105mm, the Russian 122mm, British and American 4.5in guns; British 5.5in, Russian 152mm, German 150mm and American 155mm howitzers.

In smaller numbers there were also, for field use, some useful mobile heavy guns whose chief task was counter-bombardment, and a few monsters which were really curiosities and had little tactical significance.

The Germans had one most unpleasant weapon, a 170mm gun of such high velocity that the shell arrived in advance of its noise. The Americans produced an excellent range of heavy guns and howitzers especially their 155mm nicknamed "Long Tom". The Second World War was not a heavy artillery war like the First. By virtue of range, weight of bomb and flexibility, aircraft had finally rendered obsolete the endless rows of 6in, 8in and 9.2in and even 15in guns seen in France, although the Germans reverted to the use of some gigantic guns when besieging Sebastopol in the Crimea.

We must take note of anti-aircraft guns and dismiss them, because the whole subject is intensely technical. Though this is not to say that they were not extremely important. Radar, analogue computers, electronic laying and fire-control, tachymetric sights were all in being or developed during the war, and by 1945 the Germans had made a breakthrough into surface-to-air guided missiles. The development of aircraft as a battlefield strike weapon which could virtually paralyse unprotected ground forces naturally led to a demand for AA defence, but this, tactically speaking, is a separate subject, too long to include here.

The German 88mm FLAK (anti-aircraft) made a sensational debut as an anti-tank gun. This was really because all the armies made the same wrong assumption about tank warfare. The field guns, which were one of the primary objectives in a tank breakthrough, were trained to look after only themselves, while the infantry were given a "self-defence" gun small enough for them to manhandle and to be concealed easily in the forward defended localities. This was at first a tiny little cannon of 37mm with very high velocity firing a hardened steel shot. Any experienced big game hunter could have told them that when dealing with a dangerous animal at close

An 8.8 cm Flak 18 dug in in an anti-tank role in north Africa. The "88" had a muzzle velocity of 2,624 feet per second and a horizontal range of up to 16,183 yards. At 1,000 it could penetrate 103 mm of armour.

Below: A British 17 pdr anti-tank gun in action in Italy. The 17 pdr could penetrate 231 mm at 1,000 yards when it fired APDS rounds.

quarters the safest plan is to carry the hardest hitting weapon available, however inconvenient. The Germans, always bold and imaginative tacticians, dared to put their ponderous 88mm AA gun in the front line as an anti-tank gun and were able to pick off the out-ranged British tanks of 1940-1 vintage like rabbits from 1,000 or even 2,000 yards. The British used, or mis-used, their 25 pdrs in the same way.

As a result each side developed bigger and bigger anti-tank guns as artillery as opposed to infantry weapons as the war went on. The first step up was the introduction of the German 50mm and British 6 pdr; these were superseded by 75mm and 17 pdrs. Some of them,

The 155 mm Gun, or Long Tom as it was often known was developed from a design which dated back to World War I. It was however an accurate piece which could fire a 94.7 lb shell up to 17,800 yards, though the maximum range was 20,100 yards.

A British 25 pdr Gun-Howitzer in the Far East.
The 25 pdr was an 88 mm gun which fired a
variety of shells including solid shot in an anti-tank
role. It had a maximum range of 13,400 yards,
and its firing platform gave it a 360 degree
traverse.

A Bishop self-propelled 25 pdr Gun in Italy. The Bishop was a Valentine tank chassis mounting a 25 pdr Mark I.

like the American 3in gun M 10 and the 75mm PAK were put on tracked chassis. The Germans and Russians used both guns and howitzers as "assault" guns *(sturmgeschutz)*, but neither the British nor the Americans favoured these hybrids, which were really armoured fighting vehicles rather than artillery.

Self-propelled *field* guns were purely indirect fire artillery weapons designed to accompany tanks and armoured infantry and gave them indirect support.

Taming the Blitzkrieg

Organisations varied from army to army and were continually changing. The thing to remember is that the basic building brick in all armies was the "division", defined as a force of all arms small enough to be manoeuvrable but big enough to stand up for itself. Therefore in it were found field and medium guns and howitzers, anti-tank and anti-aircraft guns. Batteries were usually of four guns – three batteries to a battalion; four battalions to a division – 36 field and 12 medium guns and howitzers.

Heavy artillery and reserve artillery was brigaded; the Russians went as far as having whole "divisions" of artillery commanded by major-generals. Rommel very sensibly grouped his few medium and heavy guns together and used them *en masse* when the British in the Western Desert were having their worst fits of dispersion.

The British were the odd men out all round. All the divisional artillery was of 25 pdrs in three regiments each of three eight-gun batteries – 72 guns in all, one battery for each battalion. (They tried 12-gun batteries but this proved unmanageable.) Reserve 25 pdr regiments, mediums and heavies, were organised into brigades called for some reason "army groups, Royal Artillery" – inevitably "AGRAs". In the AGRA was at least one medium 5.5in regiment per division, so in fact the overall pattern was the same as in other armies although the nomenclature was dif-

ferent. AGRAs could be used as a complete fire unit, and this proved a formidable instrument.

It is ironical that the artillery, which is fundamentally an attacking weapon and which in the earlier war had converted itself into a highly scientific arm, was forced by the blitzkrieg to act defensively until 1942, and also to throw science to the winds and fight muzzle to muzzle at close range, as our ancestors had in the days of smooth-bore cannon.

The difference between the blitzkrieg and ordinary old-fashioned, conventional tactics is the difference between American and Rugby football. The American version is methodical and guided by carefully worked "plays" or tactics. It is tough, but the game proceeds in short bursts separated by long pauses for detailed orders to everybody as to what to do next. It is very rigid and while reaching the goal is important, it is really all about making ground, or capturing territory, just like war. The blitzkrieg is like Rugby football played by an Irish or Welsh pack of forwards: the important thing is to keep the play open and moving and knock hell out of the opposition without too pedantic a regard for the rules.

In the blitzkrieg things happened so quickly that counter moves were often out of date before they could be put into action. At the receiving end the first warning the defenders had was a hurricane bombardment of indirect artillery fire plus the even more terrifying

A Russian 122 mm Field Gun Model 1931. The
122 mm fired a 50 lb shell 22,500 yards. It was a
combination of a new gun grafted onto the carriage
of a 152 mm Gun-Howitzer Model 1934, which
was introduced into service about the same time.

A 10.5 cm leFH in North Africa. The 10.5 cm light field howitzer first appeared in 1935, and served with the German army until 1945. It could fire a 33 lb shell 11,675 yards, but this was increased in later marks to 13,500 yards.

A deserted German battery near Moscow following the Russian counter offensive. The guns are 15 cm sFH 18 howitzers, they had a maximum range of 14,600 yards and fired a 95 lb shell.

attacks by Ju-87 dive bombers in depth penetrating to the field artillery areas. The main attack when it came was not by tanks alone: there was also infantry, determined to break the front and let the tanks through into the rear. Even single guns were pushed forward by hand by determined artillerymen, to open fire at the closest of ranges at the first sign of resistance. Casualties were ignored. Strong points, instead of being methodically reduced, were by-passed. The generals and colonels were right up in front, scolding the laggards and encouraging the leading troops

to get on – "get on!" (The Japanese, also bold and putting a premium on dash and courage in the attack, routed the hapless British in the same fashion in Malaya; indeed, the Japanese seem to have borrowed their attack tactics from the Germans.) It was all very disconcerting for untrained troops – or troops trained to fight another sort of battle – however brave. The greatest German victory was to roll back the Red Army, with humiliating losses, to the very gates of Leningrad and Moscow. On a miniature scale, Rommel, with a machine gun battalion, a reconnaissance battalion and a regiment of tanks, chased a bigger but badly led British force ignominiously back to the Libyan frontier during spring 1941.

Neither the British nor the Russians had much luck with their counter-offensives at first. The winter battle of 1941 in Africa ("Operation Crusader") was an honourable draw, but the planned offensive of May 1942 was pre-empted by Rommel's attack and in the ensuing battles round Tobruk the British suffered the most severe defeat in their military history and with the loss of many

guns in gun versus tank duels; 160 on 6 June alone. The 25 pdrs had been called in to redress the balance between gun and tank and, although they did nobly, not only were they defeated but they were prevented from doing their proper job. The Red Army's casualties in the same period are not exactly known, but they were certainly astronomical.

However, there were signs that the tide was beginning to run the other way. As early as Easter 1941 at Tobruk, four troops of the Royal Horse Artillery broke an attack by 5th Panzer Regiment; later that year Rommel's

A PzKw III of the Afrika Korps receives marshalling instructions as it mounts a sand dune in north Africa.

A Russian 76.2 mm Model 1939 Field Gun. This piece fired a 14.11 lb shell up to 14,500 yards. Like most guns of that period it also had an anti-tank capability. The Model 1939 was used throughout the war, though it was superseded by the Model 1942.

A 6 Pounder anti-tank gun. The 6 pdr was first delivered in September 1941, but by 1943 it had been replaced by the 17 pdr in Royal Artillery batteries but was retained for use by the infantry. It could penetrate 75 mm of armour at 500 yards and 63 mm at 1,000 yards.

"dash for the wire" when he attempted to break the "Crusader" deadlock by ignoring the 8th Army and thrusting into Egypt, was rudely halted by the gunners of the 4th Indian Division; at Alamein the 2nd Rifle Brigade with a number of the new 6 pdr anti-tank guns withstood an attack by a panzer division and killed 50 odd tanks in the course of a day's fighting. The battalion commander, Colonel Victor Turner, was awarded the Victoria Cross. From the British point of view the threat of the blitzkrieg was finally liquidated on 6 March 1943, when Rommel inadvisedly launched two and a half divisions against their position at Medenine. The RAF and the light anti-aircraft guns took the sting out of the preparatory Stuka attacks; as the panzer regiments advanced the field and medium ar-

tillery hit them at long range, stopping some attacks altogether and disorganised others; and, when the German tanks closed, the 6 pdr guns and the 17 pdrs took a deadly toll. After a day's fighting and losing one third of their tanks the Germans withdrew, leaving the British in possession of the battlefield without loss of one tank or gun. In some ways Alem Halfa where Rommel was checked the previous year was more of a watershed for the 8th Army, but Medenine was like a laboratory experiment designed to test the tank versus gun equation.

These little battles in Africa were significant, but they were operationally only small beer. The great, decisive battle was at Kursk on the Russian front in July 1943. "Operation Citadel" was Hitler's own idea,

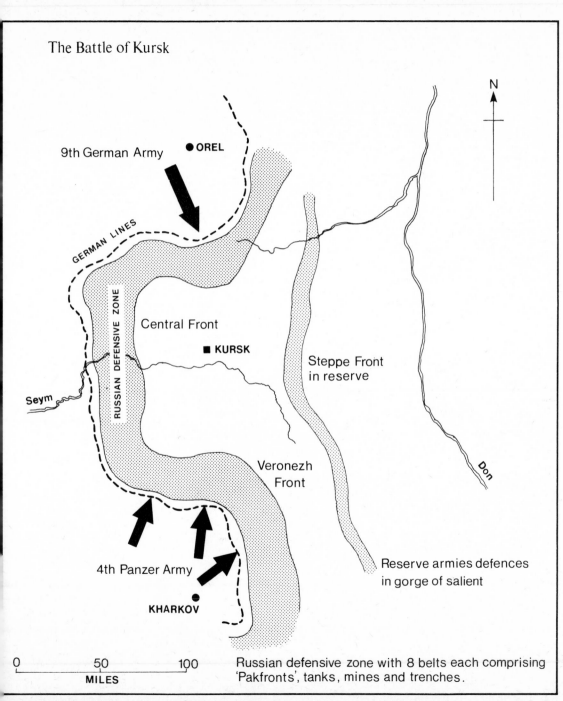

The Battle of Kursk

9th German Army

● OREL

GERMAN LINES

RUSSIAN DEFENSIVE ZONE

Central Front

■ KURSK

Steppe Front
in reserve

Seym

Veronezh
Front

Don

4th Panzer Army

KHARKOV

N

Reserve armies defences
in gorge of salient

0   50   100
MILES

Russian defensive zone with 8 belts each comprising
'Pakfronts', tanks, mines and trenches.

The Battle of Kursk, or "Operation Citadel" was the German's last attempt to gain the initiative in the East. Their tanks were defeated by massive fortifications, deep minefields and heavy artillery fire. after the German attacks had been stopped the Russians went onto the counter-offensive.

A Soviet 203 mm Howitzer. This piece fired a 220.5 lb shell 17,504 yards. It travelled in two loads, the barrel on a wheeled or tracked carriage and the carriage and recoil mechanism on its own tracked carriage.

An American 155 mm Howitzer. This howitzer
fired a 95 lb shell 16,000 yards. An accurate and
popular weapon it was first developed in 1939 and
by 1945 some 4,035 howitzers had been built.

A Russian 57 mm anti-tank gun in position during the fighting for the Kursk bulge in 1943. The 57 mm gun could penetrate 140 mm of armour at 540 yards.

intended to unlock the stagnated Eastern front once and for all. His plan was to make a huge tank attack to cut out the westward jutting Kursk salient. Altogether 17 panzer, three panzer grenadier and 16 infantry divisions were to be thrown into battle, using many of the new Panther and Tiger tanks. The German general staff were against the offensive as, among other things, many of the troops lacked training, the new Panther tanks were still suffering from defects, and the same old tactics

were going to be used, for which the Russians were now quite prepared. The blitzkrieg relies on its novelty and its almost hypnotic effect. Once the defenders gained confidence, ignored the threat to the rear and discovered how vulnerable tanks really were, the old reckless *élan* had to be modified.

On their side Russian intelligence had early warning of the offensive and under the guidance of General Zhukov prepared a phenomenal artillery defence, organised in great depth, so that the attackers having pierced one position found another behind and so on for mile after mile. The Russians have always been great believers in the value of numbers, and in planning estimated their strength in the number of artillery pieces per mile of front. There were actually more artillery regiments by one and a half than infantry regiments; 9,000 additional pieces were moved to the expected German thrust line, or 92 regiments. Some 6,000 anti-tank guns were dug in, the batteries echeloned behind each other, with defending tanks positioned to manoeuvre in the gaps.

The Russian plan was not at all defensive. It was first to bring the assault formations under a terrific indirect fire bombardment; then to let the panzers break themselves on the anti-tank defence (which included 4,000,000 mines) and subject them to heavy air attack. Only when the Germans had been very severely mauled, and had begun to withdraw, were the Russian tanks to be let loose. "Citadel" was a great disaster for the Germans. It lasted from 4 July, when after the usual brief hurricane bombardment and air attack the panzers rolled into the attack until 13 July, when it was called off. On 18 July Zhukov began his counter-offensive with two tank *armies*. Such was the scale of the fighting.

For ease of organisation the huge mass of reserve artillery in the Red Army was organised into artillery divisions and "shock artillery brigades" which could be sent to any threatened sector or, after Kursk, concentrated to provide the intense bombardment required to ensure the breakthrough in the subsequent offensives. It was all very crude. Communication was by telephone and the favoured tactic was the preparatory bombardment. Not until mid-1943 did Artillery General Semenov suggest that it might be possible to use the artillery barrage as covering fire, instead of stopping it

before the assault began. To say this is not to denigrate the Russians. They created a victorious artillery arm in the middle of a great defeat, using the simplest methods to suit the men and material they had and they could justly claim that they were the master gunners of the Second World War. The British Royal Artillery might dispute this, on the grounds that better organisation and applied science made their fewer guns more effective.

Soviet gunners leap to man their 152 mm Gun-Howitzer during the fighting for Belgorod. The gun has the light weight spoked wheels fitted for horse traction.

A Soviet 122 mm Field Howitzer Model 1938. The
Model 1938 fired a 47.98 lb shell up to 12,909 yards.
It was the standard divisional and Army
howitzer throughout the war. Captured models
were used in some numbers by the Germans.

An American 105 mm Howitzer M2A1. The gun could fire 13 different types of ammunition and was placed on a variety of mobile mounts. By the end of the war a total of 8,536 had been produced.

A British 5.5 inch
firing during the
winter of 1944. The
"five five" had a
maximum range of
16,200 yards and
fired either an 80 lb
or a 100 lb shell. The
gun was popular, and
despite its size was
employed as a direct
fire weapon against
bunkers in the Far
East.

Speed, Simplicity and Science

Whatever may be thought of Marxism as a philosophy it has one great military virtue – it encourages its followers to think things out from first principles. When the great Zhukov said in his reminiscences that the "Party" had helped him, an uneducated ex-sergeant of cavalry, to solve military problems, he meant it. Artillery was the correct solution; there was no argument, no ridiculous jealousy between arms; all officers regardless of arm must understand its use, and its command was exercised by lieutenant and full generals. Not so in the British army, whose officers are more intuitive and rarely intellectual. Infantry and cavalry (armour) remained supremely and deliberately ignorant of a science any VI form boy with a little physics and trigonometry could understand. Worse, all the lessons of the First World War were thrown out of the window. British theorists were obsessed with memories of the Battles of the Somme and Passchandaele with sad lack of logic, as if artillery had caused the disease instead of being a symptom. (General "Strafer" Gott, responsible for many of the self-induced defeats of the British 8th Army, was obsessed with the need to avoid the pounding tactics of the Western Front.) For 18 months in the African campaign the artillery effort was dissipated and misused. The 25 pdr field batteries, instead of being massed, were sent scurrying hither and yon in ones and twos, or were deployed as anti-tank guns to make good the deficiency caused by the lack of foresight and understanding which had left the artillery without a suitable gun until 1942, when the 6 pdr came into service. The British tanks were similarly undergunned until the Americans provided them with 75mm gun Sherman. It is well worth noting that the Russians did not make the silly mistake of arming *their* tanks with a pop-gun. Their rigorous analysis showed them clearly the tank for what it was – a closefighting armoured gun platform which existed solely to carry the biggest gun they could mount.

For two years the Royal Artillery beavered away developing techniques its obscure leaders knew would be wanted sooner or later but, and as is always the case in history, the time has to be ripe for reforms and the right man has to be present. The right time proved to be the summer of 1942 and the right man was an infantry officer called B.L. Montgomery. Montgomery was only an original tactical innovator in the British army in that he actually believed in thinking things out. He saw that in Africa he would require a reorganised artillery arm usable as a united weapon system. Accordingly he sent "for the best Gunner he knew", who was Sidney Kirkman, then only a brigadier, and told him to prepare for the Battle of Alamein.

The British, unlike the Russians (and to a certain extent the Americans), considered that artillery fire should be covering fire. (There is

A German 15 cm sFH18 towed by a 12 ton Sd.Kfz.8 semi-track. The howitzer fired a 96 lb shell up to 18,163 yards. The Italians and the Finns were supplied with 15 cm howitzers, and the piece was put on a tracked chassis as the *Hummel*.

A British 5.5 inch gun in the Far East. The gun was developed in the mid 1930's from a specification for a gun that could fire a 100 lb shell 16,000 yards. The production model could not only fire 16,000 yards, but also reach 18,500 yards with an 80 lb shell.

a sound old tactical adage "that there should be no movement without fire and no fire without movement".) Its aim was not to destroy but neutralise the defender's fire and so keep its own infantry alive while moving into the close combat phase (what Montgomery called the "dog-fight"). Two techniques lay ready for this, left over from 1918 – the only difference being the speed at which they could by now be arranged. One was the creeping barrage – a dense belt of fire behind which the infantry advance at about 100 yards in three minutes, aiming to keep so close to it that they are on top of the enemy positions before the fire has lifted. The other was a carefully arranged programme of concentrations of fire lifting according to a timetable. Usually there was a combination of the two, and smoke producing shell was mixed with each technique if the weather conditions were favourable.

At Alamein in 12 days' fighting 1,000 guns, including 176 mediums, were used under centralised control at the decisive points of attack and they fired 1,207,000 shells. The enemy positions had been closely studied and the featureless desert carefully surveyed. There was no preliminary bombardment: the huge and intricate programme was fully "predicted" and came down with a simultaneous crash never forgotten by those who heard it on either side. The only concession to "preparation" was a fierce counter-bombardment programme fired for 15 minutes before zero on the Axis artillery; this was according to a highly developed, scientific technique (totally ignored on-artillery men until they actually came under enemy shell-fire) which had been put aside after 1918 but carefully kept alive in the British School of Artillery at Larkhill in case it was needed.

An American 105 mm Howitzer firing in Normandy in 1944. The piece was widely used, and some 8,536 were produced during the war. It fired a 36 lb shell up to 11,000 yards.

These great programmes of fire still took at least hours or even a day or two to prepare; there were endless calculations and all the extra ammunition that had to be brought and dumped. How was centralised control on this scale to continue to be exercised in the rapidly changing turmoil of a modern tank battle – the "dog-fight"? This problem seemed insoluble and there was endless argument about it. It took a simple-minded genius to persuade the orthodox in their relentless pursuit of accuracy that accurate fire was of no use if it was late, and anyway what was the point of pinpoint fire in the kind of battle when the target – a squadron of tanks, for instance – covered four times the area of a football pitch?

General A.J. Parham, as he became, based his method of fire-control on three propositions:

1. The whole secret of modern fire-control lay in *connecting the observers, the command posts and the artillery commanders on a single radio net* where, if good discipline and economy of speech was enforced, decisions could be taken and orders given in split seconds.

2. Any gunner worth his salt could *spot a target on a modern map to 100-200 yards* each way by eye. Every battery was ordered to lay on it.

3. *Trust the man in front.* There was to be no tedious passing back of information to command posts far in the rear for earnest debate about allocation of batteries and ammunition.

Any one of a row of captains either in tanks or carefully sited on commanding ground with the infantry normally wielding the fire of his own four guns was allowed, in an emergency, to cut loose with a whole division of artillery, 72 guns or more. For a big, planned battle a more senior officer was sometimes sent forward with the special mission of bringing down concentrated fire, but experience soon showed that the seasoned captains and majors of the Royal Artillery, keeping the closest touch with their tank and infantry friends (with whom they lived, day in and day out, and knew personally) were able to send back a stream of information of how the battle was going which was back at division HQ in minutes. Such a system had existed in embryo before, but the technical side was slow and complex involving a series of elaborate mathematical conversions. Parham short-circuited this by inventing a system of fire-control orders that could be applied without conversion to every battery, and so childishly simple that on one occasion in Africa he halted an American artillery battalion sent to reinforce him and, sitting on the road-side, showed them in five minutes with pencil and paper how to interpret British orders.

A 25 Pounder with crew in text book positions during a visit by the King in 1941. By 1945 12,000 guns had been built and it had served in every theatre. A reliable weapon it was used as an anti-tank gun in north Africa as a stop gap measure.

A Taylorcraft Auster Mk IV. This aircraft was fitted with a 130 hp Lycoming P-290-3 engine. The Auster was an inexpensive, but reliable aircraft capable of operating from rough airstrips and even fields. It gave artillery officers an AOP, Aerial Observation Post, with a wide command of the battlefield.

The other idea of Parham's, which the US Artillery was quick to adopt in a big way, was another revolutionarily simple one – the "air observation post". He was an amateur pilot and he asked himself why Gunner officers could not learn to fly cheap, elusive light aircraft which could land on a pasture or even on a road, and thus provide themselves with a mobile, aerial observing platform which could climb to 500 or 1,000 feet to obtain command and dive down again out of sight. To fly, to operate a radio set and pick up and engage targets seemed a lot for one man to do, but it worked, and the combination of the two simple systems proved able to find targets and bring down a hammer-blow of artillery fire at a moment's notice to soften resistance or break up a counter-attack. (Thus under Royal Artillery auspices was born the present British Army Air Corps.)

Command Systems

In artillery tactics there are, and always will be, two violently conflicting demands. To obtain maximum effect the artillery weapon must be wielded as a whole, but this can involve delays while conflicting demands for support from the combat zone are referred back to HQ. To obtain a rapid reaction the combat units demanded the permanent attachment of batteries located close to them and whose officers are accustomed to working with them. Indeed, the Russians, Germans and Japanese all went so far as providing artillery companies as part and parcel of their regiments, worked by infantrymen. These cannon companies were eventually replaced by mortars, but the principle is the same.

Each great army reflected in its artillery system its national characteristics. Typically the Japanese set little store by it, their secret of victory being infantry of suicidal devotion; *banzai* rather than bombardments. The Red Army operated a huge artillery arm controlled rigidly from the top. The British ended the war with a powerful artillery arm but their ratio (and the American's) was, roughly, a third of the infantry strength overall plus reinforcing medium guns on the scale of about 16 per division, about a battery per battalion. The Russians often deployed more artillery regiments than infantry regiments on the *schwerpunkt*.

The Americans, as might be expected, were thoroughly businesslike and "managerial".

The organisation for command was very like the British, but with one important difference. The forward observers were junior officers whose task was to pass demands for fire from the infantry, describe the target and adjust it. How many guns were to engage, and with how many volleys, was decided in the fire direction centre far away in the rear. In this way, they thought, priorities could be assessed and the best use made of the guns. It was a rigid system, not permitting the instant reaction the British infantry expected when a fire plan went wrong or an unexpected enemy weapon cropped up and was causing

A 15 cm sIG 33 Heavy Infantry Howitzer on a range in Germany in 1940. The piece was intended for close support, it could fire smoke and HE up to 5,140 yards.

casualties. The Americans were highly efficient, more deliberate and more authoritarian than the easy-going British, and their system was necessary in an army which had expanded from almost nothing to one as big as the German army. Everyone had to know the sacred "standard operating procedure" (SOP) and stick to it on pain, if not death, of a severe kick in the pants.

The British system was different because while both the other armies were professional the British were incorrigible amateurs. The artillery arm had been neglected because it was "scientific" and the artillery officers themselves were divided between those who preferred polo to ballistics and a tough-minded minority determined to restore artillery to its proper place on the battlefield, to borrow Winston Churchill's phrase. It therefore had to wrestle within itself to hammer out a proper doctrine and then when this was agreed, to sell the idea to a reluctant armoured corps and the uneducated infantry; an extraordinarily unmilitary and unbusinesslike way to set about things. Fortunately the facts of geography allowed the

An American gunner cleans the bore of the 105 mm Howitzer mounted in an M4 medium tank chassis. This self-propelled mounting gave the piece greater mobility and some protection to the crew.

British army two years' grace to modernise it-self and the final answer, agreed by all, was the fastest, most flexible and the most responsive.

Some post-war critics maintained that as a result the British came to depend altogether too much on their guns, and indeed in the 1950s there was a marked reaction against what some armoured soldiers and infantry regarded as a reversion to the bad old doctrine which the French expressed as "l'artillerie conquiert, l'infantrie occupe" – "artillery wins the battle and the infantry occupy the ground". But it must be remembered that the British army, unlike the Germans and the Americans, entered the war without a proper main battle tank with a big gun and without adequate air support for their ground combat troops. The doctrine of the Royal Air Force centred on strategic bombing, it had neither the intention nor the correct aircraft for the task of supporting the ground combat troops and nearly three years elapsed before this was remedied.

The war the British fought was predominantly an infantry war, in which no

A battery of 10.5 cm leFH 18 howitzers caught by Soviet forces of the Kalinin Front. Though this howitzer looked archaic with its large spoked wheels it was an efficient piece which could fire a wide range of projectiles.

British commander could afford casualties on the scale accepted by the Russians, Germans or Japanese. Every ingenuity, therefore, had to be employed to preserve the lives of the infantry from enemy fire – better to waste a 1,000 shells than one precious rifleman. No battle better exemplifies this ingenuity or this lavishness than the 8th Army's attack across the Wadi Akarit, 6 April 1943. The German-Italian position consisted of a very strongly defended anti-tank ditch; the flanks were secured by the sea at one end and some salt marshes at the other with two formidable mountain features held in strength acting as

bastions in the centre and left. The attack was by three famous divisions; the 51st Highland Division on the right, the 50th in the centre and the 4th Indian on the extreme left. By this date the barrage had returned to favour and could be used in the most flexible and ingenious ways, as map 2 shows. The Highlanders used five barrages in three phases all in different directions to suit the infantry plan, and one actually changed its direction, making a swing to the left. The infantry assault began in the dark, guided by the guns marking out the opening line with a standing barrage on which they were able to form up and align

A 5.5 inch gun is towed out of the Tunisian mud. The 5.5 inch entered service in 1941, and was first used in north Africa.

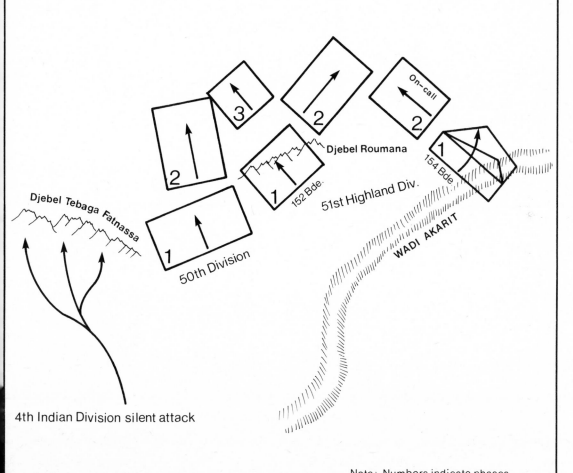

Wadi Akarit

The 8 Barrage Fire Plan

(Timed and on-call concentrations omitted)

Djebel Roumana

Djebel Tebaga Fatnassa

152 Bde.

51st Highland Div.

154 Bde.

WADI AKARIT

50th Division

4th Indian Division silent attack

On-call

Note: Numbers indicate phases

themselves. Thereafter 40mm Bofors anti-aircraft guns fired bursts of tracer over the heads of the infantry on the bearing of the advance. There were altogether no fewer than four zero hours. The fifth barrage was called for by code-word. All moved at different speeds, according to the ground and the infantry plan. This was one of the most complicated fire-plans successfully to be executed.

On the left under General Tuker, a former Gurkha officer and one of the ablest tacticians the British army has produced, there was no barrage. It would have been impossible to use one among the jagged spires and ridges of the Jebel Fatnassa rising hundreds of feet above the plain. He elected to assault as soon as it was dark in complete silence and without artillery support – but not without an artillery fire-plan. Tuker and his artillery brigadier (Ken Dimoline, one of the very few territorial

A troop of 40 mm Bofors anti-aircraft guns firing on a range in England in 1943. The Bofors gun was first produced in Sweden in 1930, and by 1939 it had been exported to 18 different countries.

Top Right: A 25 pdr Mark 2 on a carriage Mark 1 with its gun limber.

Lower Right: A review in 1941. The 25 pdrs are being towed by 4 × 4 Quads, a tractor built to take six men and fitted with lockers for 96 rounds.

gunner officers to reach this rank) had worked out a fire-control system of their own, similar to Parham's, if not quite as flexible. All the likely targets were chosen in advance and were plotted on tracing paper or marked on the maps of the junior commanders leading the attacking units, and each was given a number or a code-name. All the artillery data was worked out in the command posts in advance. The plan was to allow the British, Indian and Gurkha troops of this highly skilled division to infiltrate the enemy positions in silence, and "take them out" with kukri, bayonet, grenade or rifle as convenient, only calling for artillery fire when the assault troops were finally stuck. The great difficulty in an assault up a mountain in the dark is to discover one's own position. For this the 4th Indian division had invented an ingenious solution. All the targets on the map trace were, of course, identifiable by their map-references. On demand the LAA 40mm Bofors would fire a burst of tracer at a designated target, enabling at once a puzzled company commander or artillery observation officer to orientate himself in the dark.

Tuker's assault and triumphant capture of

A German soldier cleans a shell before loading a 15 cm howitzer. The crew are part of a battery in position on the Mediterranean coast in September 1943.

the horrific Jebel Fatnassa position belong to the saga of the infantry. It is however worth recording that his gunners, on receipt of a radioed code-word from the artillery captains in the infantry fire fight half way up a mountain in the dark, blasted the defenders with 21 artillery concentrations. Some of these con-

centrations were by single regiments (24 guns) but some were as big as 96 25 pdrs and 16 5.5 guns.

Tuker disliked barrages on principle; he considered that they dissipated fire-power and negated the battle-craft of his skilled infantry by forcing them to advance in rigid, regular lines. All the same, when he was virtually responsible for the fire-plan of 6 May 1943 when the 4th British and the 4th Indian Infantry finally broke the Axis position in Tunisia, he used a barrage with 304 guns on a frontage of 3,000 yards with another giving depth. Counterbattery fire was on the scale of ten friendly guns to each hostile one, fired in bursts. The 25 pdrs fired 386 rounds per gun in 24 hours. After the barrage had carried the assaulting troops to the first objectives the plan reverted to Tuker's favoured method of pre-arranged concentrations to be called for by radio. This was artillery support on truly Russian scale made possible by advanced gunnery and an elaborate radio network.

It is worth noting that this fire-plan was augmented as soon as it was daylight by 2,000 sorties by bombers and fighter-bombers.

From this date onwards the pattern of artillery employment remained the same as the scale increased. Tactics became a matter of statistics. For operation "Veritable", on 8 February 1945, the 30th British Corps had to blast its way through the "Siegfried" defences with "no room for manoeuvre or scope for cleverness" as the Corps Commander put it. The fire-plan involved 1,050 pieces of artillery plus 466 non-field artillery – tank guns, anti-tank guns, LAA, mortars and machine guns – plus 12 32-rail rocket projectors (a weapon which, like mortars, the conservative Royal Artillery has never fancied). Eleven thousand tons of ammunition were dumped in preparation for the battle.

It is of great and abiding interest to note the conclusions of post-war operational research

German paratroopers fire a 10.5 cm L.G. 40 recoiless gun. The gun could fire a 32 lb HE round or a 25 lb hollow charge round. The crew are standing to the side of the gun to avoid the back blast.

A U.S. gun crew fires a 155 mm self-propelled gun at a German bunker near Grossenich on 16 November 1944. The Americans discovered that with a 155 they could destroy bunkers with three rounds while remaining out of range of small arms fire.

Soviet 122 mm Field Howitzers Model 1938, some of the guns which bombarded the defences around Berlin in April 1945.

concerning these vast bombardments. An intensity of 1,000 field and medium shells per hour per square mile seemed enough to keep most of the enemy inside their shelters; double this ensured total neutralisation, but after this increases in intensity did not pay a dividend in terms of decreasing the casualties inflicted on the assaulting units.

In the South-East Asia theatre artillery languished; partly, as has been said, because the Japanese obtained their startling successes using intimate close support from light artillery and mortars; partly because of ineptitude, as shown in the Arakan the British offensive of 6 January 1943; and partly because of the defeatist assumption that the terrain was unsuitable for any but light guns. (It was quite true, of course, that mountain ranges up to 10,000 feet clad in dense tropical rain forest do not in any way resemble Salisbury Plain.) This was put right during the revitalisation of the army in India undertaken by Giffard and

An Italian civilian gets a free tow from a Quad towed 25 pdr.

Below: A 25 pdr Mark 2 on a carriage mark 2. It has been fitted with a muzzle break after the experience of using the gun in an anti-tank role. The axle is narrower to allow the gun to be Jeep towed.

Slim and implemented by a number of exceptionally able artillery brigadiers familiar with the latest European techniques. One of the three divisional regiments was re-armed with 3.7in mountain howitzers and 3in mortars, and the 25 pdrs were made more mobile without degrading their performance by shortening the axles to enable them to negotiate narrow jungle tracks.

As in Africa there was a reversion to close-range direct-fire work; the target now being not the tank, but the "bunker", and the role

Dressed in windproof smocks and equipped with rucksacks men of the Mountain Artillery Regiment man a 3.7 inch howitzer. The howitzer could be broken down into man or mule portable loads.

not offensive but defensive. The Japanese soldiers could go underground like moles and given a little time could build a fortification of earth and logs almost invisible in the jungle and proof against almost any high explosive projectile smaller than a 5.5in. They were sited with fiendish cunning so as to give mutual support, and exacted a terrible price from the infantry in the Arakan fiasco.

Tanks and flame-throwers were an effective answer, but often the bunkers were only accessible to artillery. The technique used was to blow away the foliage with 25 pdr HE to reveal the target and then, invoking eighteenth century siege craft, to construct a

A 2 pdr anti-tank gun fitted with side shields. After mid-1942 these guns were used only in the Far East where they were effective against Japanese light tanks and fixed emplacements.

A 75 mm pack Howitzer in the snow in Italy. The 75 mm had a maximum range of 9,760 yards and fired a 14½ lb shell.

battery and "arm" it in the dark to bring point blank fire to bear. The favoured weapon was the 6 pdr anti-tank gun which was taken to pieces and brought up bit by bit by hand and assembled in a pre-constructed gun pit, this operation itself required covering fire. As soon as it was daylight fire was opened with armour piercing shot on a loop-hole, to enlarge it, followed by HE.

On occasion a 5.5in was used from about 500 yards firing delayed-action HE "direct", with sensational results. The 5.5s were also used "indirect" with good effect, but with very slow results, not that this mattered because war in the jungle is a slow process.

Loading and firing a 7.2 inch Howitzer.

Top: Carrying a 202 lb shell in its cradle.

Bottom: Loading the shell, on the left a gunner waits with the bagged charge. The 7.2 inch Howitzer had a maximum range of 16,900 yards.

For more formal fire-plans there was a reversion to "artillery preparation", the aim being to destroy, not neutralise, as many bunkers as possible in advance. Then neutralising fire had to be kept up during the assault until the infantry were 10 yards from their objective, not 100 yards as in other theatres: the infantry forming places were often only 50 yards from the objective. A typical plan started with the preliminary bombardment which lifted to fresh targets in depth to isolate the objectives as soon as the

Top: the 25 lb charge is placed in the breach. The crew are men of the 2nd Army in action in North West Europe in September 1944.

Bottom: the howitzer fires. The recoil forces of the 7.2 inch howitzer were too heavy for the carriage and so heavy timber coins (wooden ramps) were positioned to take the recoil. The piece can be seen rolling back up these coins.

A 15 cm sFH 18 abandoned outside Leningrad in January 1944. The gun position is littered with ammunition boxes for the charges.

infantry signalled their readiness to jump off. As soon as they did, direct fire weapons or tanks took over with capped (delay fuse) HE, then AP and finally machine guns, at the last possible moment. On one occasion at the battle for Kohima a cloudburst blotted out the target area and the tanks continued to fire blind while the assaulting troops, Gurkhas, unaware that they were now inside their own supporting fire continued to advance to find the Japanese still pinned in their bunkers.

They killed 40 out of 60 Japanese and took the position almost without loss.

Broadly speaking all the advanced methods used in Europe were applied in India and Burma, the only difference being that the problems of supply and transport cut down the amount of ammunition available. There was no question of dumping thousands of tons of ammunition and plastering the landscape with shell-fire in the hope that all enemy positions, detected or undetected, would

Soviet gunners load their 203 mm Howitzer Model 1931 (B-4). This piece was mounted on a tracked carriage. It fired a 220½ lb shell to a maximum range of 17,504 yards. The howitzer went into six different variants, but with the exception of the first piece they have similar ranges.

The biggest weapon in the Allied armoury, the 240 mm gun. The piece was broken down into loads that were towed by converted M3 medium tanks. A 20 ton crane was used to assemble the gun. It could fire a 365 lb shell. Guns such as the 240 mm were however giant freaks in World War II.

somehow be hit. For instance in New Guinea, to take an extreme case, it once took 20 porters all day to bring 20 rounds of ammunition four miles from supply point to battery. This meant extreme economy of means and ruled out the creeping barrage. In February 1945 it was only possible to maintain 90 guns forward to support the two attacking divisions, 20th Indian and 2nd British, crossing the Irrawaddy river instead of the normal 144 25 pdrs which would have been available in Europe plus the usual group of mediums and heavies. Nevertheless, by using the divisions in alternating phases and giving each one the full support, the obstacle was successfully crossed in the face of determined Japanese resistance and so successful was the counterbombardment programme that the Japanese artillery was suppressed for 48 hours.

As the 14th Army advanced in central Burma it reached open country and tactics became more European in their nature. The Japanese, without armour, without air support and with hardly any artillery, were incapable of anything except a dogged withdrawal with halts for a suicidal defence. The artillery task therefore became more and more that of an eliminator of strong points. Failure to do this could be very expensive indeed, for the individual Japanese soldier remained unshaken. General Stilwell's staff had no idea of artillery tactics or technique, with the result that a weak brigade of Japanese infantry, many of whom were sick or wounded (or both), held the town of Myitkyina for some two and a half months when besieged by the US trained Chinese army. In the amphibious operations in the Pacific the United Stated forces, both Marine Corps and Army, after a costly landing at Tarawa deployed an immense fire-power, which included both air support and the guns of the US Navy, in their relentless advance from island to island.

Above: A German battery commander's H.Q. on the Western Front in 1939.

Right: A 40 mm Bofors light anti-aircraft gun in position during a large scale exercise in England in 1943.

The Lessons

Warfare remains an unpredictable activity. Before 1939 military analysts had predicted dominance of strategic bombing, the obsolescence of artillery and the likelihood of wars on land being decided by manoeuvre. This was only partly true. The decisive influence of air-power proved to be not the bombing of capitals but in cooperation with armies and fleets. The blitzkrieg was mastered and battles on land were decided very much in the manner of 1918, with all three victorious armies deploying a huge artillery arm in support of what were, fundamentally, still infantry operations.

Military historians should stick to the record and leave military "lessons" to the instructors at staff colleges, although the past has in this connection marked relevance to the future. Thirty years after the blitzkrieg had faltered and then broken under British and Russian guns the technique was brilliantly revived by the Israelis. Once again in 1973 the tank soldiers, exhilarated by a series of runaway victories, rashly concluded that the tank was the queen of the battlefield and all other arms, including the artillery, were its maidservants; once again, with historic irony, under Russian schoolmasters, the tank soldiers were taught the same lesson as the Germans had learnt in the Steppes. The Israelis are now reviving their artillery arm.

There is an old-fashioned children's game, now forgotten, called "zogging". (In a more adult usage Royal Navy officers played it to see who would pay for rounds of drinks in their wardrooms.) Finger gestures, made simultaneously, signify "paper", "scissors"

A 25 pdr at full recoil. It is being used in the mortar role to fire shells at a high angle.

Soviet gunners of the 2nd Baltic Front manning their 122 mm Model 1938 howitzers during fighting in 1944.

and a "stone". The paper wraps up the stone, but is cut by the scissors, and the scissors are broken on the stone. This is a tactical parable. Unsupported tanks are broken on guns (or, today, anti-tank missiles); missiles can be taken out by infantry or suppressed by artillery; infantry can be overrun by tanks. Each arm by itself is both weak and strong; all three acting united and in sympathy are unbeatable. When both sides know this lesson, then the outcome of the battle is decided by courage, skill-at-arms and numbers interwoven in a subtle equation. Artillery remains the cement of victory.

THE FIELD ARTILLERY FAMILY OF WEAPONS

The Russians on the one hand and the British, Americans and Germans on the other all had different equipment policy. The westerners tried to rationalise their inventory so as to simplify ammunition supply and spare parts, training and so on, whereas the Russians deployed over a dozen varieties of weapon including mortars of 160 mm. They favoured guns, treating them as dual purpose HE field guns and shot-firing anti-weapons; the westerners preferred howitzers. The British were under-gunned with their main weapon, the 25 pdr, but had they adopted the 105 mm howitzer instead, as some advocated in the early 1930s, they would have been virtually defenceless against tanks. This table is not meant to be exhaustive but to enable weapons to be compared.

British	United States	German	Russian
88 mm	105 mm howitzer	105 mm howitzer	105 mm howitzer
"25 pdr" ("gun-how")	36 lb shell	33 lb shell	also
13,400 yds	11,000* yds	11,675, increased	122 mm howitzer
		to 13,500 yds	52 lb shell
4.5 in gun	4.5 in gun		12,700 yds
(114 mm)	See British	105mm gun	
55 lb shell		33 lb shell	12 mm gun
20,500** yds	15 mm howitzer	20,860 yds	50 lb shell
	95 lbs		22,500 yds
5.5 in ("gun-how")	17,800 yds	150 mm howitzer	
(140 mm)		96 lb shell	152 mm howitzer
100 lb shell,		18,163 yds	90 lbs
16,000 yds			18,700 yds
80 lb shell,			
18,500 yds			

*NB These are maximum design ranges. The fighting or "planning" range is effectively about 75 per cent of the above
**This gun fell out of favour owing to its inaccuracy at longer ranges, and because the 5.5 proved so excellent a weapon for all purposes.

These were backed up by smaller numbers of mobile heavy guns and howitzers; e.g. the British 7.2 in howitzer (202 lbs/16,900 yds), the German 210 mm howitzer (250 lbs/18,263 yds), the US 8 in (203 mm) howitzer (200 lbs/18,510 yds) and 240 mm howitzer (360 lbs/25,000 yds); the US "Long Tom" 155 mm gun (95 lbs/26,000 yds), German 170 mm (138 lbs/32,375 yds).

GUNS VERSUS TANKS

This is a rough guide for comparison, showing how performance was successively improved. The performance is indicated by the thickness of armour in mm penetrated by a solid shot. All tanks were vulnerable to direct hits from HE by 25 pdrs and near misses by 5.5 in guns, and artfully sited guns firing from a flank. The first Tiger Pz Kw Mk VI captured by the British fell to a 6 pdr.

Gun	Army	500 yds	1,000 yds	
37 mm	British and German	36	27	Also in US service.*
2 pdr	British	53	40	
45 mm	Russian	60	38	
25 pdr (88 mm)	British	62	54	
50 mm	German	65	53	A great killer of British tanks.
88 mm FLAK and adaptions for field use	German	112	103	First used in 1941, over a year before the 6 pdr came into service.
6 pdr	British	75	63	146 mm with APDS.
75 mm	German	171	130	A very good gun, but short lived.**
76.2	Russian (also used by the Germans)	90	83	Deadly. Sometimes mistaken by British for an 88 mm.
17 pdr (76.2 mm)	British	123	113	231 mm with APDS.

All of the above were mounted in tanks except the Russian 45 mm and the 25 pdr as well as on SP A TK tracked mountings. At the end of the war the Russians introduced the 85 mm, which was also a tank gun, and the 100 mm.

* the US inventory was similar to the British but, except for the debacle at Kasserine and Sidi Bou Zid, the Americans never had to face a panzer onslaught on a grand scale.
** supplies of tungsten carbide for its special shot ran out.